Ocean Adventures

The Southern Ocean

Written by
Sadie Hallworth

KidHaven Publishing

Published in 2026 by
KidHaven Publishing, an Imprint of Greenhaven Publishing, LLC
2544 Clinton St., Buffalo, NY 14224

Written by: Sadie Hallworth
Edited by: Noah Leatherland
Designed by: Ker Ker Lee

Cataloging-in-Publication Data
Names: Hallworth, Sadie.
Title: The Southern Ocean / Sadie Hallworth.
Description: Buffalo, NY : KidHaven Publishing, 2026. | Series: Ocean adventures | Includes glossary and index.
Identifiers: ISBN 9781534552098 (pbk.) | ISBN 9781534552104 (library bound) | ISBN 9781534552111 (ebook)
Subjects: LCSH: Antarctic Ocean--Juvenile literature. | Marine ecology--Antarctic Ocean--Juvenile literature.
Classification: LCC GC461.H355 2026 | DDC 910.9167--dc23

Printed in China

CPSIA compliance information: Batch #QW26KH: For further information contact Greenhaven Publishing LLC at 1-844-317-7404.

Photo Credits – Images courtesy of Shutterstock.com, unless otherwise stated.

Cover & Recurring – Oleksandr Matsibura, Nastya Vaulina, alazur. 2–3 – Pekinnaird. 4–5 – Kingppin, Islandjems - Jemma Craig. 6–7 – juan68, Stu Shaw. 8–9 – JMP_Traveler, ManuMata, Rainer Lesniewski, max dallocco. 10–11 – CherylRamalho, Petra Christen. 12–13 – Ekky Ilham, Tarpan. 14–15 – Pataporn Kuanui, Valery Evlakhov. 16–17 – Jeremy Richards, Lomvi2, CC BY-SA 3.0 <https://creativecommons.org/licenses/by-sa/3.0>, via Wikimedia Commons. 18–19 – robert mcgillivray, GTW. 20–21 – CherylRamalho, Oleksandr Matsibura. 22–23 – juan68, LouieLea, Danita Delimont.

CONTENTS

WORDS THAT LOOK LIKE THIS CAN BE FOUND IN THE GLOSSARY ON PAGE 24.

OCEAN ADVENTURES

We are going on an ocean adventure! Hoist the anchor and let's set sail. Let's start our journey by going over the basics. Oceans are large pools of salt water. Earth has five main oceans.

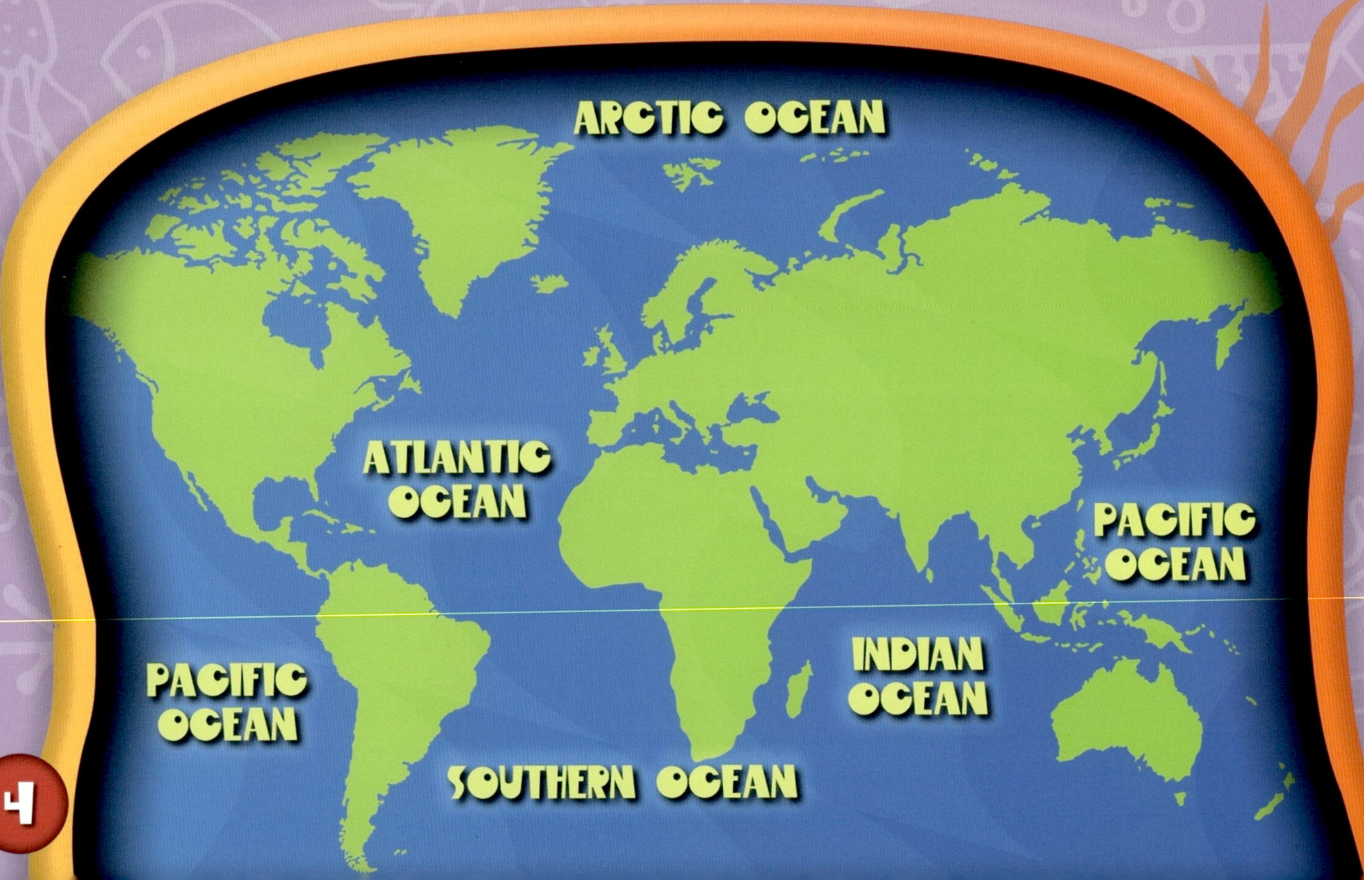

Oceans are home to lots of life, including plants, animals, and other living things. Oceans help humans too. Oceans help make the air we breathe. They also help to control the planet's temperature.

HEALTHY OCEANS ARE IMPORTANT FOR THE HEALTH OF PEOPLE AND THE PLANET.

THE SOUTHERN OCEAN

Dress warmly! We are visiting the Southern Ocean. The Southern Ocean is around Antarctica, which surrounds the South Pole. It is connected to the Pacific, Atlantic, and Indian Oceans.

The Southern Ocean is known as the newest ocean. The body of water has existed for a very long time. However, it was only given its own name in the 2000s.

EVEN BEFORE IT HAD A NAME, SCIENTISTS KNEW THE SOUTHERN OCEAN WAS UNIQUE.

STUFF TO SEE IN THE SOUTHERN OCEAN

The Drake Passage

The Drake Passage is the thinnest part of the Southern Ocean. Strong currents here make it very dangerous for explorers. The Drake Passage was named after an explorer called Sir Francis Drake.

The Antarctic Convergence

The Antarctic Convergence, or the Polar Front, is the outer edge of the Southern Ocean. This line marks the place where the temperature gets much colder. The colder water is perfect for Antarctic wildlife.

WEATHER

The Southern Ocean is very cold. It has strong winds and lots of storms. These cold winds are very important. They help control the temperature all over Earth.

The Southern Ocean's strong current moves cool water around and pushes it into other oceans. This strong current is called the Antarctic Circumpolar Current. It is the strongest current on Earth.

PLANKTON AND KRILL

Phytoplankton

Phytoplankton are tiny pieces of algae. Many animals eat phytoplankton. It is very important for ocean ecosystems. In summer, so much phytoplankton grows in the Southern Ocean that it can be seen from space!

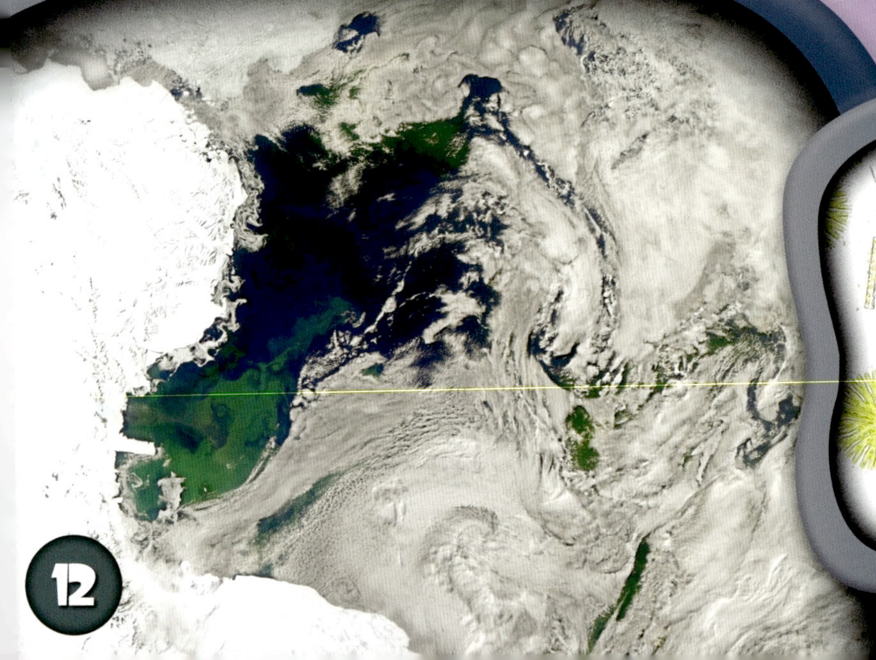

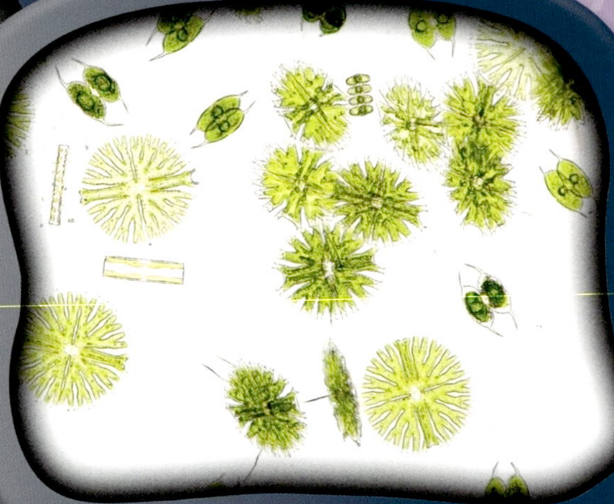

Krill

Krill are tiny, shrimp-like creatures. They may be small, but they are very important. Many animals eat krill, including penguins, seals, and whales. Without krill, these animals would not survive.

FISH

The Southern Ocean is so cold that most fish cannot live here. Some fish have adapted to cope with the cold. Fish that live in the Southern Ocean have special blood that does not freeze in the very cold water.

Icefish

Many animals have red blood, but icefish have colorless blood! Since colorless blood carries less oxygen, icefish have big hearts to help them move the oxygen around their bodies better.

MAMMALS

Hourglass Dolphins

Hourglass dolphins are some of the only dolphins that can live in the cold waters of the Southern Ocean. Dolphins live in groups called pods. There are usually 10 to 15 dolphins in a pod.

Southern Elephant Seals

Southern elephant seals are the largest seals on the planet. They are excellent divers. They have a thick layer of fat called blubber. Blubber keeps the seals warm in the cold water.

BIRDS

Wandering Albatrosses

Wandering albatrosses spend most of their time flying over the Southern Ocean. They even sleep floating on the water. Wandering albatrosses have the largest wings of any bird.

Wandering albatrosses can glide through the air without flapping their wings.

Emperor Penguins

Emperor penguins live on the Antarctic ice. Unlike most birds, penguins cannot fly. Instead, they are excellent swimmers. Emperor penguins can dive deeper than any other bird and stay underwater for over 20 minutes.

On land, penguins live in large groups called colonies.

OUR CHANGING OCEANS

The Southern Ocean is changing because of climate change. Climate change is causing the water to warm up and the ice to melt. Lots of Southern Ocean animals need ice and cold water to survive.

The Southern Ocean helps keep Earth cool. If the Southern Ocean keeps warming up, so will the planet. We can all help protect the Southern Ocean by learning more about climate change.

LEARNING ABOUT CLIMATE CHANGE IS THE FIRST STEP TO SOLVING THE PROBLEM!

EXPLORING THE OCEAN

Exploring the oceans is a great way to learn more about our world. If we dive down deep enough, we could discover amazing new animals or interesting objects from throughout history.

Which Southern Ocean animals would you like to meet? Would you like to dive deep with the emperor penguins or elephant seals? Perhaps you would prefer to soar above the sea like the albatross?

GLOSSARY

adapted changed over time

algae plant-like living things that have no roots, stems, leaves, or flowers

climate change a change in the typical weather or temperature of a large area over a long time

currents movements of water in one direction

ecosystems everything that lives together in an environment

temperature how hot or cold something is

oxygen the natural gas that many living things need to survive

unique one of a kind or unlike anything else

INDEX